Faith In The Eye Of The Storm

Faith In The Eye Of The Storm

By

Willie Randolph

Dedication

I would like to thank God for my life, health and strength to be able to stand and continue to move forward with a voice of Compassion, Unity, and Unconditional love for all mankind. Because of HIM I move, breath and have life to share my Test that hopefully will be a testimony that others will be able to grow from.

I would also like to thank my Mother Grace Jean Randolph (RIH) who instilled my belief in God and my Faith in HIM. Truly, it wasn't her saying you must follow this that made the difference in my life, it was the example she lived every day that allowed me to see the difference between True Faith vs Seasonal Faith.   Because of her and my siblings Yolanda Randolph,   Justina Boone, Steven Weston and countless relatives, true friends, peers, and family support and Unconditional Love I share this book with you.

Contents

Foreword

Almon W. Gunter Jr. CEO/President Almon Gunter Motivates

As an avid sports fan, motivational speaker and author I have had the opportunity to realize many of my dreams as well as inspire and others to achieve his or her dreams. There is no greater feeling than mentoring, coaching, and serving others in the game of life.

Willie Randolph has done a marvelous job in writing a book on relying on faith over fear. His straight forward approach provides useful information that can be applied immediately to help you to rely on faith no matter the storm.

Faith In the Eye Of The Storm is an exciting book filled with incredible stories that will help you connect the dots to trust in God. I encourage you to read the following pages with an open mind and a willing heart to bring about any change you want in your life. You have all you need to achieve your goals on the inside of you.

Willie has written a superb presentation on never giving up and to always choose faith over fear. So enjoy every page, stay focused, and above always maintain Faith!

Introduction

On Monday, the 22nd of August, 2005, students from all over the world and vastly different walks of life began pouring into the University of New Orleans campus for the start of classes. Some were getting ready for their first year in college, and they had all the enigmatic excitement of being a new college student. For others beginning their final semesters, soon, they will say farewell to a University that housed and educated them for three years prior. Whatever the varying positions, all students were thrust together in one beautiful sea of camaraderie. New roommates would meet, and new friendships would form, some lasting for the rest of their lives, and others dwindling at the end of the school year. But the experiences would last forever, good or bad.

As these young scholars, writers, businesspersons, teachers, mathematicians, scientists, and athletes arrived on campus and began unloading their gear, a hurricane was brewing thousands of miles away. None could have realized at the time, but that weather pattern, seemingly so separated from their lives, was

4

going to smash into the Gulf of Mexico with a level of destruction like no prior hurricane. On the 29th of August, one week after the beginning of the semester, the storm would not only bury the city of New Orleans in an ocean of water but consume and transform the lives of thousands of students who would come to know and never forget the name "Katrina."

I survived Katrina because I practiced the teachings of my mother, and I had faith in the Almighty God. My arrival at New Orleans stemmed from my need for independence.

In the year 1992, I got my first job as a waiter. I served diligently. This job was great for me because it helped me get through High school and got me my first car. When I graduated, I moved into the corporate world and went far south to Tennessee. Unfortunately, I couldn't stand the realization that I had to work my butt off while clothed in fancy ties and suits. I used my time after work to do some running and general fitness training. Six months down the road, I realized that 9 to 5 wasn't my thing. I also discovered that many people weren't happy with the corporate lifestyle.

I reached out to my mom. Her advice was crisp. "Why don't you be a coach?" She said. I took her advice, and I quit my job. Later, I did a part-time job, and after a short time, my coaching opportunity came.

I called Chuck Louis, and he told me about a job at Belmont University. And boom! That was how I became an assistant coach. I coached every track event from sprints to long jump, hurdles, relays, pole vault, and so on. I did this for 3 years at Belmont. Afterward, I headed to Vanderbilt for about a year. From that point, I was nudged by my friend, Jim, to move forward and go for something higher.

I applied to a couple of jobs that summer and I got my first head coaching job at the University of New Orleans. That was my first-ever head coaching job where, ironically, my AD came to Nashville and interviewed me while he was traveling.

This was how my dedication and desire for independence brought me to New Orleans that would soon be ravaged by the ugly face of Katrina.

Chapter 1

Storm on the Horizon

I set down the phone after speaking with a real estate agent about buying a home in the New Orleans area, where I had lived for the past three years. My search led to a property in Slidell, and there were a few odds and ends to tie up before making the final decision. As I closed in on a new home, my attention was beginning to shift entirely to the 2005 track and field season that was approaching.

In 2002, Jim Miller, the Athletic Director of the University of New Orleans (UNO), hired me as the head coach for the track and field team. I knew it was going to be overwhelming sometimes and would take painstaking dedication for the team to reach the mark that I had set for them in my head. It takes time, hard work, and commitment, both from your athletes and the University, to build a successful athletics program, but above all, it takes Faith. You need Faith in the school, Faith in the athletic department, Faith in the athletes, and Faith in oneself. Having been the head coach for three years now, I was preparing for what could be the best year the UNO's track and field program had ever seen. It was our peak year. We had the resources, the coaching staff, and above all, the athletes to make this season one that Louisiana would never forget.

The day was Saturday, the 27th of August, and the new athletes were gathering for their physicals in the Lakefront Arena. This was one of many structures that would be consumed by the ocean a few weeks later. Before I could head over to check on my athletes, I had an itching reminder early that morning that I needed to call my mother.

Yolanda, my older sister, who lived in New Orleans, had called before the sun came up, in her usual manner, and asked, "Have you talked to momma yet today?" I jokingly replied, "As soon as you get off the phone, I can."

Then, she asked me if I had heard about the storm. I quickly said, "No, but whatever storm it is, we are in God's hands. We can't control the weather, so why worry?"

Yolanda didn't hesitate to correct me, explaining that the storm seemed severe and that she would call later because her friend was talking about evacuating the city with their family, and she needed to find out the details. Then, when my mother answered the phone, I said, "Good morning Ms. Randolph," and she smiled through the phone, saying, "Hello Mr. Randolph." They had somehow become nicknames for us. That is our private joke of false formality. I told my mom of what Yolanda had said, and that I needed to get over to the arena and check on the students. The freshmen and cross-country athletes were undergoing physicals, and I wanted to be there to ensure everyone was getting along alright. This would be the last time I spoke with my mother extensively for several days, leaving the family, and myself, in an uncomfortable limbo of uncertainty, coupled with the intensity of the storm.

The absence of communication was painful. Speaking with my family every day was a ritual that gave me a sense of guidance, protection, peace, unconditional love, and purpose to be the best I could be, no matter the obstacles that surfaced. The complete and utter lack of communication was the most significant obstacle I would face from the moment the storm reared its ugly head, with the waters rushing over the levees and flooding into the city.

When I pulled up to Lakefront, the shadow cast from the massive octagonal arena and blanketed my black, four-door Sebring. And as I walked away from the parked vehicle, a ping of uncertainty tapped my spine. Whether it was the looming storm or because my last car, a Cutlass Supreme, had recently been stolen from my apartment complex, I don't know, but I felt it, and it was scary.

As I entered the arena, my phone began to ring. It was Trent Ellis, my jumps coach for the University's track team. Coach Ellis lived in Baton Rouge where Louisiana State University is located, about an hour outside of New Orleans. He asked if I had heard of the storm that was heading for the coast.

He said it was called Katrina.

I told him all I had heard, which was mainly faint rumors and no specifics. Ellis went on to explain that it was a massive hurricane building off of the southern coast and was possibly heading for New Orleans.

Now, this was the second time of hearing about this storm, and the startling possibilities were swimming into my head. Immediately, my mind went into survival, protection, and plan mode. Coach Ellis wanted to know if I had a plan for the athletes and if the school had been talking about the storm and the risks. I had not heard so much as a whisper from the athletic department, and because this was only my second time hearing about the hurricane within the past twelve hours, I had no plan for my team either. After I hung up the phone with Ellis, my hand was reaching out for the handle of my office door, and I knew it was time to begin. It was time to be Coach Randolph, the man who had to appear confident when everything was falling apart around him. The man who had to have the answers to the questions being asked. The man who would try to stand firm and unaffected, but a man who would be forever changed with the city, intrinsically.

My perception was vital. I didn't want to create panic about an issue that may not be as severe as the news agencies or personal conversations were attributing.

Just one year previous, a hurricane called "Ivan" had struck the coast of Louisiana with extreme intensity. People were told to evacuate, and everyone took serious precautions like:

- Fortification of homes

- Erection of shelters or creating buildings designated as shelters
- Gathering of food stockpiles by FEMA
- Clearing of evacuation routes
- Closure of schools, etc.

In the end, the storm shifted direction after crossing over the Caribbean and into the Gulf of Mexico, inevitably striking the coasts of Florida and Alabama. The storm then moved inland, causing over 100 tornadoes and merged with a frontal system over the Delmarva Peninsula on the Eastern shores of the U.S. Before the hurricane dissipated, as most do this far inland, a lower extra-tropical portion split from Ivan had drifted south into the Atlantic, over southern Florida, and into the Gulf of Mexico for a second time. There, the weather pattern gained strength over the warm waters, becoming a tropical storm; however, before reaching the coast of Louisiana, that small portion of Ivan had lost momentum and landed in the Cajun State as a tropical depression. While there was damage done, it wasn't anywhere near the predicted magnitude, and much of the preparations were in vain.

Knowing this, I decided to keep calm and check on

my athletes. At this moment, with a potential hurricane so close, thousands of students swarming together, and the University either unconcerned or uneducated on the matter, there was little I could do but be strong and positive. I said a quick prayer to God, believed he was forever by my side, and held myself up with the confidence that God was going to help me with my internal fears, fears which would grow with the progression of the day, and the circumstances of the storm.

I walked confidently through the front doors. Doors I would have had to swim through a few days later. Inside, there seemed to be no sense of urgency. There were thousands of collegiate athletes meeting with doctors, exploring the facility, and inquiring into their fellow teammates. The scene was calm, considering the massive volume of people. No one seemed to be concerned or even aware of the storm. It was the start of school, and whether it was the overwhelming excitement or lack of effective communication, the students were enveloped in jovial conversations, utterly unaware of the possible realities that lay ahead. Seeing this, I focused on my task at hand and checked to be sure our athletes were getting along well, and that their physicals were running smoothly. My priority was helping those who had recently transitioned from a foreign country.

An aspect of UNO's athletics program that always made me proud was the willingness to welcome students from all over the world, including Zimbabwe, Grenada, Guyana, Jamaica, Trinidad, Uganda, The Netherlands, and France. This hugely broadened the pool of ethnic, cultural, and traditional diversity. While it was a unique melting pot of cultures, languages, and people, there was also a possible foundation for confusion amongst these varying ethnicities.

Juggling the hurricane on my right shoulder, the army of athletes on the left, a virtually purchased home on my head, and my sister and nephew still unsure of what their plans were, I was struggling to keep balance. All I knew was that my mother always taught me to pray and trust God in the face of adversity. She trained me to never give up on loving people no matter their background and who they are but walk by Faith.

For the first time, I was honestly waiting for God's guidance. I was literally waiting for the next move. I counted on Him for the ability to show confidence before those without the same Faith and comfort. Unknowingly, my staff was soon to become the only family I could rely upon. Still, I felt I needed to rely on God for everything; because humans, the hands of men and women, were not strong enough to fix this problem, to slow down the storm, to protect all of my athletes, to give me some semblance of relief, and confidence. I felt that only God could bring those desperate needs to fruition. But the hands of those men and women who became my family, who lived by my side for the challenging months ahead, tangibly manifested into the comfort that God could never have brought, and I only had known some of them for a few weeks, or even days.

A new cross-country coach who had initially moved in with me when he first settled into the area was beginning his first year at UNO. His name was Chris Neil, and he had formerly coached at Ball State University but was now ready for a fresh start in New Orleans. When I found Chris, I asked him how the kids were doing. He had no negative news and was disturbed to hear about the storm, but he assured me that everything was going to be fine, and the kids seemed to be very calm, considering the frenzy of activity. Chris was particularly unsettled because he was from up north and had never experienced a hurricane. He now lived in an apartment next to mine; however, his moving truck had still not arrived in the past three weeks, leaving Chris in a transitional lull from Midwest Indiana to coastal New Orleans, a distance of about 860 miles.

I retreated into my office for a much needed, quiet, prayer time. I spent a few minutes crying, asking God, "Why," and if this was real. For some time, I reflected and allowed myself to feel the many emotions I had been suppressing in an attempt to appear strong. Afterward, I made a call to Eddie Nunez at LSU and asked for his permission to come and stay at his place for a few days. This was not new for us. During some of the routine hurricanes that went over the Louisiana coast, we stayed together. However, the usual relaxing atmosphere of our visit was clouded by the necessity of me seeking refuge and the potential severity of the storm. For a month, his house would become a haven for me to live and operate out of, always in communication with the kids, parents, FEMA, coaches, families, and many other responsibilities that come with running a collegiate track and field program during a severe hurricane.

After the talk with Eddie, I called Glenn Jenkins, the throws coach, into my office and told him to communicate to all of the kids and coach Neal that we had an immediate mandatory team meeting that evening. While Jenkins faithfully sought out the students and coaches to inform them of the meeting that would outline their evacuation, he had no intention of leaving the city.

Glenn Jenkins was a former Marine. He did not have the funds to leave and felt that he would be able to tough out the storm. Jenkins shared a sentiment that many New Orleans residents had; either they did not have the funds to leave, did not feel the storm would be as severe, or felt that regardless, they could weather the storm and protect their belongings. Storms had battered the coast of Louisiana for so many years and were often so exaggerated by the media who play on the fears and concerns of people. This time, the people weren't threatened. These people could have never known what was coming. No one was telling them anything, and for many, even if they knew the level of destruction Katrina would bring, there was nothing they could do. The resources were not given to help them get out of the city. This was their home.

The traditions of New Orleans ran deep in the hearts and history of the people who had lived there for generations. New Orleans is a city molded by slavery and cultured by the influences of the French, Spanish, Americans, and Africans who inhabited the humid swamplands and levee protected neighborhoods. Before Hurricane Katrina, African Americans made up sixty-six percent of the city's population. After Katrina, seventy-three percent of these people were displaced by the storm, with more than one-third living in poverty. Not just for African Americans, but all of those living in poverty before and during 2005, the option to evacuate the city, seemingly simple to those watching on their TV screens, or from comfortable air-conditioned bus seats out of foggy windows, was not so clear. The humble homes they inhabited, primarily located in Mid-City and the Lower Ninth ward, was everything they had. For many, the reality of leaving the lands they worked on and fought for was crueler than the prophetic destruction of the hurricane.

Wood, brick, concrete, plastic, drywall, metal, and

stone are all physical aspects of a house that can be replaced. What makes a home is not its materials, but the memories and sentiment it holds for the owner. New Orleans was their home, and even the smallest and seemingly inconsequential buildings they inhabited were as crucial to them as Buckingham Palace to Queen Elizabeth. Their families fought to create it, oppressors had tried to destroy it, and the descendants of those families were going to preserve it. Whether Glenn Jenkin's relationship with New Orleans ran that deep, he was joining the masses of people who would stand firm, protect their homes, secure their families, and hold on tight in the wake of what was to come. I did not have such luxuries. In my position, the option of toughing out the storm was irresponsible. The lives of 45 humans were in my hands, and even my Faith was not strong enough to keep me there. We had to act, and I needed to prepare for such action. Before organizing the students, I had to organize myself.

I started to pack my backpack with all of my folders of students' information, budgets, floppy discs with workouts, and anything I feared would be lost in the storm. I could never have known I wouldn't need all of these small intricate things, and wouldn't be back in my office for a month.

As I left my office, students immediately started coming up to me to say that many of the doctors were not going to give physicals anymore, because the parishes they lived in were beginning to evacuate the city. Moments ago, there seemed to be no whisper of this storm, and now, suddenly, people were starting to vacate the city. I was mildly shocked by this change in tone and told our athletes to return to their physical areas and wait until I could find out more information on the matter. The news was scary. The hurricane was becoming a reality. But I knew my athletes were further in the dark and closer to the edge of panic than myself.

Routine physicals are often an inconvenience when preparing for the new school year or applying for a new job. For collegiate athletes, physicals are vital. To be considered a division one athlete, allowed to practice with the team, and receive benefits such as financial aid, books, and athletic gear from the University, it is required of the athletes to complete their physical examinations. However, there was another layer to the necessity.

As discussed, many of the students arriving at UNO were coming from foreign countries. Some may have had the resources to purchase necessities such as school books, backpacks, and, for the track athletes, proper running equipment. However, the majority of these students were from impoverished areas, including some US natives. They were admitted because of their physical ability. They had a once in a lifetime opportunity to attend and compete at a division one school that their financial capabilities could not provide. To receive the resources promised to them by the University in exchange for their participation on the track and field team, they needed to have completed physicals. If they couldn't complete the physicals, they would not be eligible to compete, and they often couldn't attend the University. And now, having traveled thousands of miles, said goodbye to their families, and watched their homes fade away in the rearview mirror, these students were one evaluation away from achieving their dream and the doctors were leaving.

I knew that if we didn't have a meeting to calm everyone's nerves, some students would leave if they had the resources or suffer if they did not. The only administrator there at the time was Mike Daunhauer, so I quickly looked for him to get a grasp on the whole situation. After running back and forth from my office to the gym where the students were getting their physicals, I finally located Mike. When I found Mike, he was back in his office behind a towering wall of paperwork that never seemed to shrink. I always felt bad for Mike as he looked like one of the good guys that regularly had excessive work to do. I had watched Mike for the last few years, continually putting out fires, and being stressed over things I felt were other people's jobs. I explained that I had heard of this storm repeatedly, it was causing panic amongst the students, and I wanted to know what the specifics were, and the school's plans in dealing with the situation.

As I stood outside Mike's door with a look of relief, he responded with a look of extreme uncertainty. I could feel it, the anxiety; the confusion, the fear, it was bubbling over, it was tingling the tip of his tongue, it was gnawing at my spine; everyone felt it, everyone saw it, and I could taste it. I knew that no matter what he said, I could not divert from my plan to leave as soon as we could with the kids. Something in me just said, "Leave."

Mike was waiting to hear from the other administrators and, therefore, couldn't know if the school had any specific instructions for the faculty. He immediately set out to find someone who could give more answers. However, it was clear that he was planning his escape. Even after his assurance that everything would be alright and he would get to the bottom of it, his eyes told me the opposite, and I'm sure mine said I didn't believe a word. Everything was not "just going to be alright" unless we acted. The lack of concern and a general understanding of the conditions from the administrative staff, whose duty it was to inform and protect the students and faculty alike, worried me more than the storm itself.

It was no surprise that people were not taking the situation seriously. New Orleans had a long history of warnings. There was always the imminent danger that if a strong enough hurricane did hit the city, it would be the end. For those living in the area, this constant doomsday prophecy had slowly lost its terror until it was withered into nothing more than a distant thought. It is only human nature to avoid thinking about the worst because it is terrifying. It is much easier to push those possibilities to the periphery and pretend that everything will be fine, even in the face of disaster. Call it coping or ignorance, but until that day came, for the people of New Orleans, the prevailing school of thought was, "I doubt it will ever happen to me."

Deeper than Trent Ellis's warnings, the doctor's evacuations, and Mike Daunhauer's lack of concern, my gut was telling me something was wrong. Again, knowing the only thing I had to rely on then was my Faith in God, I went back to my office to pray. In my thoughtful reflection, eyelids wrinkled tightly shut, with hands clenched and pressed against my forehead; I heard it once more, "Leave." At that moment, I wasn't afraid. I was in a complete "Trust God mode" for even the words I was about to say to the athletes to trust me still that we were going to be okay. At times it is best to trust the opinions of experts or join the masses, but this was not one of those times. From within, in my spirit, beneath my toes and into the crumbling Earth, I knew something was not right.

While waiting for Daunhauer to return with some answers, more students were beginning to approach me. The tone had climbed further into severity, and it was becoming clear that they were scared. The doctors were not resisting giving physicals anymore; they were gone, and no matter how hard the University's administration tried to convince them otherwise, it was over. It was time to create a plan that was independent of what the University was going to do. As a cushion, I called Ellis and talked about potential solutions. Our conversation was brief and focused on executing whatever we spoke about entirely. We knew that this was something much bigger than us. He and I immediately started to talk in ways of a father protecting his family. I was not a father, but Ellis was, and while I loved my athletes like my children, I heeded his understanding of protective parenting and used that strength and knowledge to address my children, the team.

We decided that hotels in Houston would be the best place for athletes to travel quickly and safely. I gave Ellis my credit card information and instructed him to book as many rooms as possible, knowing they would fill up quickly. I would speak with the administration about reimbursing me later. Ellis promptly went to work on his end, while I attempted to get some clarity on mine. Eventually, Mike Daunhauer returned, but with very meager information.

I told him of my plans to put the team in hotels in Houston and reiterated that while Hurricane Ivan was nerve-racking, this one seems very serious, and I am not going to take any chances.

Daunhauer still did not have any answers; he neither opposed nor supported my plan. Yet, as of that moment, he seemed to be cut off from the school's communications, and my solution for answering this problem was the only one being made. Mike Daunhauer's position in the administration was mostly financial; therefore, he may not have known the answers to any of these questions. However, he was the only administrator there at the time and had to improvise. Daunhauer decided to call Kathy Keene, the Senior Women's Administrator and Assistant Athletic Director for the school. Again, I waited for answers.

Up to this point, I had not been able to turn on the TV or listen to the radio. I was solely going off of the information my staff and students were giving me, and not to mention, Faith.

After about an hour of praying and mentally taking down notes of the things I needed, my phone began to ring, and it was Keene. Once again, I explained my plan and asked what she and the administration were doing on their end. Keene had no answers. She neither opposed nor supported the solutions I had come up with, and to my knowledge, she had no solutions of her. I knew Kathy as the woman who always had a plan, especially with young kids at home. Eventually, she decided to call the Athletic Director, Jim Miller, and find out what the department's strategy was in dealing with this situation, which was becoming more and more disconnected. I waited!

It was apparent from the attitude of the administrators, and mostly what I was being told that the school had no plan. Kathy could not confirm what Jim Miller's actions would be, nor could she answer whether I would be reimbursed for the thousands of dollars needed to book hotels in Houston. Therefore, I had to go to plan B. She assured me that the President was trying to get a few buses together that could shuttle students away to safety. What I didn't know at the time was that those athletes would be a select few, and it didn't include us!

At Universities, specific athletic programs are seen

as more important than others. Often, these proclaimed, "important sports," are called revenue sports. They differ depending on the University; however, in each case, specific games are funded more heavily, and hold more value than others, because the University knows that the sport will yield the highest revenue. The revenue sports at UNO were baseball and basketball, and they would be the athletes on those buses, not mine. The track and field team was not on the University's priority list, and in many ways, I felt the attitude of the school reflected that my team and I were disposable.

This was a harrowing experience, a blatant similarity to the Titanic where the rich were saved and the lesser folks left to their peril.

As the swirling mass of desolation was building momentum over the gulf coast, similarly, it was forming and strengthening its way into the conversations of the athletes. The nervous murmurings had begun.

Just hours before, these young men and women were mingling and laughing. They had no shred of worry in their minds. But now, the reality of their situation was becoming much clearer, and it was a scary reality. Trent Ellis, Chris Neil, Glenn Jenkins, and I needed to put a quick stop to the nervous murmurings with a clear and concrete plan. So, I instructed the coaches to round up students and explain that they needed to meet in the gymnasium next to the weight room at 5:30pm. I pulled as many student-athletes as I could find together and gave them some much-needed direction. "I do not know what is going on right now, but within a couple of hours, we are going to have a team meeting, pass the word. I'll send out messages, and we will meet in the gymnasium next door with a plan on what to do."

When I arrived in the gym, the coaches were already there with the athletes. Immediately, many students informed me of their plans to either stay with friends or family. After they explained the logistics and how they were planning to travel to the various destinations, I said my goodbyes, hoping they too would find safety.

I walked further into the room and past the eager faces with a notepad tucked underneath my arm. Then, for a moment, I stood perfectly still. I asked God for help. I asked Him to give me the strength to look into their fearful eyes, to provide them with all the power I had left, and to reaffirm in their minds that I was the coach. I was in charge, and I was going to do everything within my physical and spiritual power to protect them.

First, I said those who have already made arrangements to leave the state, be it with family or with friends, need to inform me of their travel plans, where they are going, who is going with them, and how they are getting there, as other students already had done. After clearing up those who had the privilege of leaving the state, I focused on those not so fortunate. These students were mostly from other countries such as Jamaica, Trinidad, Zimbabwe, Ghana, and Granada, amongst others.

Knowing that the support of my athletic department was dwindling, I had to make it seem like we were not abandoned, that we had the support of our University. I told them we were all to meet outside of Privateer Place, an apartment complex many were already living in, at 5:00am the next morning. After gathering there, the group, including the coaches and myself, were going to pack into vehicles and drive to the neighboring city of Baton Rouge, where Trent Ellis lived.

I went over the essential documents they needed to bring with them to be safe, the workout clothes they would need, and other seemingly small but significantly vital items they needed to remember. I explained it would only be for a few days and to consider it a road trip to LSU. Most importantly, we had to stay together as a family. There could be no isolation and individualism, we were a collective group, and one's desires could never come over another's needs. At this moment, I realized I was saying the much-needed words of comfort, support, honesty, and unconditional love that my mother had bestowed on me. Positivity was the key for me, not false hope, but a positive way of thinking. I wasn't going to allow the storm to consume their thoughts and burden them unnecessarily with a possibility that could only be imagined until it was a reality. To finish the meeting, we all circled up and prayed together.

Again, I set out to find Mike Daunhauer to inform him of my plans. In his office, Daunhauer was working his way around the room awkwardly and nervously. It was clear that the worry was becoming real, and he was scared.

The only option was to keep moving forward.

Crying over spilled milk only leaves a stain, and I had to push beyond frustrations and vulnerability to get my kids to safety. It didn't matter who was right and who was wrong, who was selfish and who was selfless, I knew the decisions I made in the next few hours could be the anchor that rooted us directly in front of the broad watery chest of Katrina's force or a lifeboat to escape its leading fist. These were our kids now, so I set to work on a new plan to ensure their evacuation. Now, we had to make sure we found places for everyone to stay for an unknown period.

Omar Sunny Smith led the drive through the back roads of New Orleans, and we had five cars in all, containing all the athletes.

The thick Louisiana heat was beginning to cut as the sun crested over the ocean, welcoming with warm arms the watery hell stirring in the massive body of blue. Sweat trickled down my back, and small drops stung my eyes as I wiped the salty liquid away with the sweaty back of my hand. That feeling of loneliness crept into my spine.

For the first time in a very long time, I felt like I was the only one in my situation. The tingle of being alone, faced with a grave magnitude of danger lingered on, and it looked like I was going into a tunnel that only God could shatter for the light to come at its end. At this point, I remembered being a fat little kid that spent many hours to myself wondering what my life was about. It was then I told myself that I am more than what I look like and that I have to talk to my mom and God. So, I called her to let her know how I was feeling. We prayed, and she assured me that we would be alright. "Just trust God," she said.

Though surrounded by thousands of students, teachers, coaches, and administrators, I felt only a few were telling me anything. My coaching staff was trying to keep me informed and ask questions, but they too looked to Coach Randolph for answers, and the people I relied on for direction were silent.

Having already spoken with the Assistant Athletic Director at LSU, Eddie Nunez, I'd made arrangements for myself and Chris Neil to stay at his place. Ellis opened up his home to many of the students, and so did numerous teammates whose families lived in the city. The plan was set in motion, and the students went off to pack and ready themselves for a scrambled and hectic day of travel.

As if there were not enough factors working against

the team that night, Chris Neil's belongings, which he had been waiting three weeks for, arrived at his apartment. Neil worked all night unloading the U-Haul, frantically trying to get his belongings into the safety of his home, before the team left the city. As the sun came up, he was unpacking the final boxes from Indiana into his new Louisiana apartment, and he made the caravan on time. Chris's labors were in vain. The apartment building that I had lived in for two years, where Neil now had a small apartment that he was frantically furnishing, would be dismembered, and underwater upon their return.

So much of the tireless work we did in preparing for the storm and protecting our belongings was, in the end, pointless! We could never have grasped the destruction Katrina would bring. All the inhabitants of New Orleans quickly saw the apathy which nature carries, working independently and unforgiving of the emotions and efforts of humans.

By 5:45am, the 28th of August, all of the teammates that were leaving together had gathered outside of Privateer Place. It was time for the University of New Orleans track and field team to go. The students and staff piled into their vehicles, and the caravan of six cars pulled out and away from Privateer Place, a building standing tall and strong in the rearview mirror, but would be reduced to rubble when they returned. Baton Rouge was 65 miles away, a drive that usually takes one hour, however not that day. When it became clear that with each meter we drove out of the city, the sky turned a shade darker; there were no longer any doubts that what I had heard from the news was for real. This was not anything like the exaggerated version of the report, which we thought it was. The predictions were frighteningly correct this time, and we had no choice but to step on the gas pedal and gain speed to safety. Before we moved the next thirty meters, the sky had turned completely dark, and the slight drizzles of rain showed us that this was no time to save the gas but be on full speed. Our headlights came on, and before long, the wind had increased its speed. I had last experienced a hurricane as a kid when I had a very faint idea of what was happening. I had seen footage of what it could look like on TV screens, but what was happening in front of me as we found our way out of the danger zone was immensely frightening. The force of the wind picking up speed practically slowed down our movement to the lowest level. The trees were bending to the power of the wind, which had nearly reached the 50 meters per hour mark.

During this time, the skies were grey, but there was nothing that looked like a major storm was about to hit. While driving, I made sure we didn't talk about loss, we listened to all types of music and sang oddly enough. Considering that I had a Jamaican, a Ghanaian, and a Ugandan in my car, I just asked about their homes, and how it was to live there. I figured that I should talk about the good things and their families as I had talked about my upbringing and family. Then I received a call, the call that would make me extremely uneasy about what to do concerning what we were discussing, my family. It was my sister calling me again to say that her plan to leave with her friend and son had fallen through and that I need to come back and get them. At that time, stuck in a mass of back roads and traffic after the fourth hour, I knew I couldn't turn around to get them. I had to figure out how to get her and my nephew out of New Orleans safely or at least communicate how I could help. As I pondered on what to do, I received a call from my mother. She was upset and asking what I was going to do to help my sister. I remember feeling my chest starting to hurt because I was holding in way too much. The burden was becoming exasperating. So, I asked the athletes to pray and that we should sing some old church hymns as I internally prayed to God to help me with what to do to help my sister, nephew, and the caravan of students following me in my car to Baton Rouge.

I did the best I could to calm the students with me and get them to see that things were going to be okay. But with what was going on as we sped out of the city, some were beginning to disbelieve me. Although I tried everything to show that I had everything in control, my mind was in a state of turmoil. The call came again from my sister once more, and I assured her I was not going to let any of my family members come to any harm. I had mentally calculated that on dropping the students over at Nunez's house, I would go back for them that same day. The car they needed to use to leave the city was grounded, and seeing people leave the city in such a hurry contributed to their sense of panic and fear. I resolved that I was going back for them, no matter what it could cost.

Through hard and rigorous driving, meandering through the hordes of people fleeing from impending danger, we made it to my friend's place in a record five hours. Another problem seemed to arise. How will 45 persons be holed up in a house that had not more than four rooms plus the sitting room? However, that being the least of my worries, I spent the rest of the evening doing my best to apportion sleeping spots to the individuals. Some parents who knew their children were in my care came along and picked them up, thereby reducing the strength to about thirty. I spent the entire night figuring out how to make it back to New Orleans for my sister and her family.

When I told Nunez of my plans, he looked at me like I was crazy.

"You mean you are going back to New Orleans? Aren't you watching the news and the forecasts?"

"It's my family. I can't leave them helpless."

"Do you see the magnitude and the scaling of that hurricane? The wind could even throw your car off the bridge."

Not wanting to be further dissuaded, I picked my car keys and made for the vestibule. He was staring at me, but he knew he couldn't stop me. He had already had enough dealings with me to understand my willful nature. He only talked because he felt obligated to do so. He knew that he couldn't change my mind. He had gotten used to my go-getter attitude soon after we had met and worked together while he was still with us at LSU during the track and field championships. We were coaching a team of eight athletes for the season's athletics meet, which would qualify us for the regional finals later in the year.

At the blast of the pistol, Denzel, our lead runner in the relay, shot into a quick lead, widening the gap with each stride of his long, sturdy legs. Just before handing the baton to Byron, he twisted his ankle and fell, much to the chagrin of the team, but based on the training they had received, Byron made up for the speed deficit, picking up the baton and completing his bit, and my team finished second. Even though the hundred meters dash was slated next and Denzel was our point-man, I was determined to field him, and no protests from Nunez would make me change my mind. The boy said he was fine, and that was it. He ended up breasting the tape first, and almost beating the school's time record.

As I reversed out of the house, I knew what I was

up against. The wind was howling and whistling through the trees at a blistering hundred meters per hour. If it was like that here, I could only imagine what would be happening in neighboring Louisiana. But that was my family, for the love of God. There was no way I was going to leave them out there when I knew there was something I could do to help them.

I put a call through to my sister.

The line was hazy, and I could hardly make out any sound.

I gunned the throttle, muttering prayers under my breath, begging God to help me to meet them alive. The drive ought to last a minimum of five hours, but by this time, the roads were free because much of the evacuation had been done, and I made it to Louisiana in three and a half, my car hugging the way at nearly a hundred and sixty kilometers per hour. When I got to the fringes of the town, I could not make out much sign of life. Things had gone awry, and I saw two massive trees fallen on some houses, causing considerable damage. I tuned up my prayers as I sped to my sister's house.

Now, the cyclone would shore up speed at some point, and ebb after a few hours. It would go up even higher the next time, and carry on in that manner. When I got to their house, there were two crumbled houses next to theirs, and it was a sheer miracle theirs was not involved. Huddling them and their belongings into the car took a short thirty minutes. They were grateful for the help, and as I was engaging the drive gear to leave, the howling wind began its destructive wave. It took all my expertise in driving to keep dodging falling trees and the greenery that was hurled before me to obstruct my vision. The rain which had suddenly begun increased tempo, and when we got to the Patson bridge, we saw to our horror, the water had risen more than ten feet, and was encircling the pillars holding it higher and higher. Thankfully, the road was clear, and I was grateful I had a sound car. I made full use of it, hitting a hundred and eighty on full throttle. Amid intermittent prayers and church hymns, we safely made it to my friend's house in one piece.

We watched what we could of the catastrophe that happened in New Orleans from the news. The people who had made light of the forecasts were the worst hit. It was difficult to believe that there were people who felt that the forecasts were mere propaganda meant to displace them from their homes. When they had realized, it was too late, and the collapsed bridge made any effort at escaping gross futility. Power lines buckled and collapsed, buildings shook to their foundations, and the streets became filled with clothes and rubble belonging to houses which had collapsed, and which the wind had blown out and away.

By the third day, we were in tears as aerial footages showed the town wholly submerged by the water, beginning first from the bridge, charging violently towards the residential areas, and swallowing it up in a consuming force. When the lights from the town went out, we knew it couldn't get worse than this.

We spent the rest of the days settling in. It was a challenge managing the horde of people under one roof, at least for as long as it lasted. The facilities were never enough, and feeding was overstretched. The students who had their parents living in Baton Rouge were able to leave after reuniting with their parents and siblings, and that reduced the numerical population of people under the roof a bit.

Gradually, because the town of Baton Rouge was

the closest to Orleans, it became somewhat of a resort, milling with people all day long. Before long, the government's relief agency began to arrive with assistance and relief for the displaced people, and we took advantage of all that they had to offer.

During this time, much of the moral burden was on me to provide direction and comfort for the students under my care, especially the international students who had nowhere to go. I had moments of near-nervous breakdown because of the trauma of seeing people injured, displaced, and homes reduced to wreckage right before my eyes. That was apart from the numerous fights and fisticuffs that come with having too many people living together. Hardly did a day pass without me getting reports of altercations between some of the children, and I was always on hand to weigh in on the matter and resolve them amicably. I depended on God for strength and wisdom, and He never failed me. At a point, I wondered if I was the one braving through this alone, with no one to turn to. It was unbelievable that I could weather the storm of fear and despair days back and cater to the children. I settled every matter that came before me to the satisfaction of each party involved.

Even Nunez could not help complimenting my mettle at handling them and was even more shocked to understand that I had not known these students more than three months before now.

Gradually, things began to ease up, and after a few weeks, the floods began to die down, as we learned from the news. The government agencies then set a period of reconstruction and rehabilitation of the city, as well as a concise assessment of the level of damage along with a program of recompense to begin immediately. In the house we stayed, the population reduced considerably in the coming days when government efforts became more accommodating of people, and other persons began to get wind of the whereabouts of their relatives and family. That was how we sailed through the difficult times together, and I have God and my mother to thank for all of what He did for me throughout that grueling experience.

Chapter 2
Stubborn Faith

I would say that I surprised myself, coming out of Hurricane Katrina stronger and better. During that period, I saw the intense power of love and how important it was to show it. I saw what Faith could do during terribly contrary situations. There were times when it looked like this was the end of the road, but my stubborn Faith in what I knew God could do helped me to pull through, and it is one of the most important messages I want to give to the readers of my story. Faith works, and I would always cherish the chorus of "Prayer Changes," by R.Kelly because the entire narrative of that song was the full story of my life at that point, and many times afterward. I saw prayer work.

Chorus - Prayer Changes

Somebody just look back over your life and
See where he brought you from
How many of you know?
Prayer changes (I heard that)
Prayer changes (I believe that)

Prayer changes (I know that)

Prayer changes things

Prayer changes (I heard that)

Prayer changes (I believe that)

Prayer changes (I know that)

Prayer changes things

Prayer changes (it changes)

Prayer changes (oh it changes)

Prayer changes (I'm a witness that)

Prayer changes things (said I know)

Prayer changes (it changes)

Prayer changes (it changes)

Prayer changes (I'm a living witness that)

Prayer changes things

But about this time, I had a severe issue. As New Orleans was picking itself up from the misery and carnage that it had been subjected to, it looked like it wasn't over for me yet.

The danger in New Orleans had reduced, and the town was undergoing rehabilitation, but that automatically meant I was out of a job. The entire University had been battered and damaged by the raging winds and torrential rain, and everything about it had to begin from scratch. I had to set about looking for ways to fend for myself, as the load on Nunez reduced considerably. I had no home at this point, so I had to rely on him until I could find my feet let alone stand on my feet. It was not like I could not feed myself days after the disaster, but it weighed me down to be a kind of liability on my friend after having gone through so much together. So, I immersed myself into joining the relief efforts of the government, volunteering to go to the neighboring city to take care of displaced persons, providing both physical and material sustenance to as many as I could during the day, and returning home to rest in the evenings.

During this period, a lot of what had been instilled in me as a child came into play. I realized that humans were the same, regardless of their race, creed, beliefs, and inclinations and deserved an equal amount of love and compassion from everyone. I did things for them not out of duty to my fatherland, but because they were victims of circumstance who were thrown into such states by fate, and I realized it could have been anybody, even me. So, with that thought in mind, I spared no effort in making sure I did my best to alleviate their pains and discomfort, radiating love and warmth everywhere I could. As I was doing relief missions and got immersed in it, I traveled with humanitarian teams around the world. I went to Fiji with AIA Athletics in action to help with their mission trip for one month. Upon my return I was offered and accepted a job at the University of Louisville.

Because I was doing things for the people at that time from within me, not expecting any reward, I soon became so engrossed in showing love to people that I forgot all about the sorrow and trauma of the hurricane some months back. I did the work for about a year and a half before I got another job at Michigan that could pay my bills and give me a stable life.

I had returned from work one day, about three years after the hurricane, and was lounging in my balcony that evening when I got a disturbing phone call. It was a doctor's voice, who asked for my identity concerning a certain woman. When I replied in the affirmative, he informed me that the woman, my mother, had been admitted into the hospital, and was in a critical state.

It shocked me because I had spoken to my mom only a few days before, and she had been hale and hearty, showing no correlation to the condition attributed to her that I heard over the phone. Promising to come over as soon as I could, I hung up, and even as I prepared to take the necessary permission from work to travel, I could not understand why God was allowing this to happen to me at this time. It was a trying period, a turning point for me.

When I got to the hospital, it turned out that things were worse than what the doctor said. My mom had been going through some intermittent sicknesses over the years, but this was a whole new level. She had been diagnosed with congestive heart failure, and she had been admitted two days past. She had degenerated into a coma, and the doctors had been doing all they could to stabilize her. First, I had to do what I could for convenience's sake, to bring her to my base in Michigan, for her to remain close and on hand with me.

I could not help but break down in helpless, weakening, and terrible tears. There I was, seeing my world, my pillar, my strength, lying down peacefully with her eyes closed, looking far off without a care in the world, with the oxygen mask on her face giving her that frightening, medical look. But this wasn't going to be for long.

Chapter 3

A Woman of Faith

Being from a sound Christian background, my mom instilled solid Christian values in us. I believe that this was what shaped and kept me going through the turbulent times of Hurricane Katrina. It was such an experience to see homes crumbling, people helpless, and children destitute, especially in the first few days in the wake of the disaster.

My mom was one of the foremost African American women to work in the post office in her community. It was such a feat at the time, another confirmation of what a firm believer in Christ could achieve. She was an inspiration to the black ladies in her time. She helped them rise above mental and societal barriers. All of these were fallouts of her implicit faith in The One who could make us do all things by His strength. She had so much love for God, and it reflected in her relationship with the people around her.

I came of age to understand the toll her selflessness had taken on her health, and I immersed myself in praying to God to help me give her the best of life in her later years, the way she deserved. I think it was this passion that burned within me for her that earned me the privilege of having a power of attorney over her. I made the best use of that position, making sure no one slighted or undervalued her all of her days.

One of the most profound influences of having Faith came from my mom. She was one of a kind when it came to professing her faith verbally and putting it to work. There have been countless instances where I watched her faith stretch beyond limits, but she would hold on, and it would eventually pay off. One such case was the period in the life of our family when it seemed like the world would came crashing down on us. She was low on cash; the bills were piling up and being the breadwinner of the home; it was such a trying time. This would have been an ample opportunity or justification for her to give in to the advances of the many men who were willing to revitalize her financial state at the time, just for a little compromise as they would love to say it. But being the Amazon of faith like she was, she would always decline. Each time she called on God for supplies, the answer came almost instantly. This made me begin to look twice at the idea of trusting

God in prayers, and before long, it began to pay off for me as usual.

There was a day she was down to her last cent. The bills for the month had been settled, but providing food for that day was not forthcoming. She resorted to prayers and trust in God, believing that the God she trusted would not leave His own to suffer. And believe it or not; the answer came precisely one hour later! Someone just knocked on the door and said, 'Hey, I know you guys are here, and you just might need this portion of food,' and that was it.

My mother was such a giant of faith, and it played out in countless situations as life went on. There were times we would hear loud praying and crying from the direction of her room. When we left the house one after the other, we could, or I, in particular, sense the force and effect of her prayers. Many situations changed due to her faith and prayer. 2 times in particular:

1. When my brother was sent to prison on trumped-up charges.
2. When I had difficulty graduating from school.

Inclusive of other troubles in our family life, her prayers caused everything to change for the better.

This was one of the first inspirations I had as a child – to take prayer and faith in God with seriousness and commitment. I applied it six years before her death when she was having health complications. I prayed like never before, and before I knew it, her health began to stabilize, and she became as well as new. My sister had taken her to the hospital that night because she wasn't feeling too well. One of the most important things my mom taught me was that I should never leave a loved one alone in the hospital because the authorities needed to know that there were people who loved and cared for the victim. I had gone there, and there was so little I could do but pray. She was lying there, hanging on to a thin thread of life. It pained me deeply and I wept uncontrollably.

I recall getting into her ward that day and holding her hands, which felt so cold and clammy, indicative of an adverse condition. I also remember the look the caregiver gave me, which signified that I needed to leave the room, but I knew right then that there was no way I would leave that room. I was so confident in my prayers, and this kept me at odds with my siblings, who had different views and subscribed to the doctor's advice. Over the next few days and weeks, things got worse. She could not breathe well and because of her condition, the oxygen could not reach her brain. Because of the lack of oxygen to her brain mom would most likely be in a vegetative state for the rest of her days. The doctors recommended that she should be removed from life support. They also informed us that in seven days, the plug would be pulled, and if she didn't breathe well on her own, she would probably be in a vegetative state.

Even though I was the youngest child, I was given a power of attorney, and I decided to have her wait on God, and it paid off in the end.

I exercised my Faith, believing God for the best, while watching her health, with firm hope that things would improve. But things got worse before it got better. It was a testing period of my life, and it was one that showed me that Faith in God was a personal matter. There is nothing called collective Faith. When you believe something or exercise Faith for a particular thing, you would be tested on it on a personal note. Looking back now, this was to form a core pillar and growth in my knowledge of God and His ways.

I remember the confidence I had and being

adamant about my faith in God and her condition. I did not give life, and I was confident in the Giver of life that He would come through for us.

While questioning my authority to take a crucial decision in my mother's life, I had to call in the family lawyer to explain the situation of things and why it was my call to make. I told them in no hazy terms that only God had the right to take life when He wills, and that no one else had that right. That was the right thing to do, and that was what I believed my mom would have done. That occasion provided me the opportunity to understand that there was a difference between talking faith, and walking it, or making Faith practical. It also made me fulfilled to realize that I was exhibiting what I had learned from my mom and not what even the church taught me. It was so disheartening to see that people could easily give up on someone when the person is down, but if the tables were turned, it would not be the case. I had received so many calls from other family members asking me to rescind on my decision. These were people I had seen my mom held on for, make sacrifices for, and do a lot of unbelievable things for. I remember she had used her last dollar at times to feed some of these people, help them find jobs, work her body sick to fend for some of these people, and it pained me that these were the same people asking me just to let her go in that manner. I saw it as an opportunity to trust God more and keep the stubborn Faith in Him.

I watched in hope and Faith and ceaseless prayer to God at this period, even as my other family members had gone to the level of sampling gravesides and appropriate burial measures and paraphernalia for my mom. It threatened to discourage me, but I did not allow it, and I continued to cry to God not to put me to shame before these people, but to give me that testimony that my mom had always epitomized.

The day finally came when the doctors were to pull the plug. The memory is still as fresh as ever. I remember vividly the sound of the plug being pulled, the refreshing surge of the air go back to her body, and how she breathe well and effortlessly on her own. The tears of joy on my eyes were indescribable as I just muttered thanks to God for helping and vindicating me before my family members. From that day, her healing came on stronger and stronger, and even though she would not eventually walk on her own, she was able to do some great things by herself. She would come to church, sing, worship, and even encourage the youth of the church at that time. She was such a reason to glorify God even in the eyes of other people, a real testimony indeed.

After she became well, one of the beautiful parts of her testimony was that I felt so blessed watching her standing on the church podium testifying to all on Sunday in the same dress that was bought for her burial! She was saying that this dress was bought to wrap her in, but she was wearing that same dress, alive and testifying. The feeling of confidence and faith I had in God and His word from that day was second to none. She even said that they predicted that she would turn to a vegetable, but she ate vegetables, the very thing they said she would become. That was the point in my life where I decided that moving forward; I was going to trust the Almighty God to the end.

Six years after this episode, I heard that she had passed. It was difficult to believe, even though I got some form of premonition of something about to happen. It did not occur to me that it had to do with my mom. According to the reports, she had just closed her eyes, and it was all over, and it was not even something serious that ought to cause death. It was only a sprained ankle that rehabilitation and physiotherapy would have easily solved.

Her funeral was a meeting point for everyone she influenced in several ways. Everyone spoke of her goodness and how lovable she was. Her favorite quote was to 'trust the Lord with all thine heart and lean not to thine own understanding' as written in the third chapter of the Book of Proverbs. Her funeral got so many people yearning to have a deeper connection with God. People ran to the altar just beside her casket. Many persons were inspired to know more about God at her funeral. It was the first funeral I had ever seen with such religious drama and passion. She was a real example of faith being more than just a verbal claim of what is hoped for, but a substance of whatever we trust God for.

Overall, I am satisfied and humbled to be a part of a generational legacy of faith in God that began from her mother. Her mother is still alive now at about 95 years of age, and her life more than ever inspires me to take over from where she stopped in her relationship with God. She put all of us in a challenging position where we would be inspired to carry this fire of faith with us and infect other people with it. And that is the point I am at right now, where I want to let the world know who my mom was and how influential she was in my life.

The bottom line of the life of my mom is - 'If one was connected to The Real Source of life, faith, and sustenance, then there is no reason to fret and worry about the issues of life because He can take care of them.'

Chapter 4

Building Relationships in Troubled Times

One of the profound beauties of life is that amid turbulence and trouble, positive things could still happen. There is always the possibility of unexpected goodness and blessings that can make one forget, or at least temporarily erase the sorrow that burdens us at such an unfortunate time. I met several people during these trying times that strengthened my faith in humanity. The impact of their influence at such a period cannot be quantified. We were burdened on every side, yet these people soothed our pains and made things easier to bear.

The church at LSU is one of such organizations. Amid the rejections and abandonment, they rekindled an assurance in me and my team of the existence of people who were still obstinately selfless and reflected the tenets of the Christian life in its most practical terms. They gave me a haven when it seemed like all hope was lost. The church at LSU wasn't big in terms of size and facility. But this church treated us kindly and put their facilities to optimum use for our convenience. Everything we needed to do as a team was catered for owing to the benevolence of the church. For a church that was so small that they didn't even have drum sets, it is such a remarkable thing to do. The love just oozed out naturally, not a love that was there because of what one could get or what the other party had, but only love that was unconditional, pure, and free. There were times we could not get on the track because of some issues, and the pastor was always there to offer us moral and spiritual support. I would forever cherish the relationship I shared with Pastor Drew, and I will surely include his church in my mentions. It is such a breath of fresh air to see people who are such a departure from the norm of doing things because of immediate or even future gains; Pastor Drew struck me differently, and I would forever remain grateful.

Coach Jenkins is another pleasant personality whose virtues shone through this trying period like a light in a dark tunnel. The worth of having someone like him around me in a time like this became more and more evident as events unfolded, and our plight worsened. Loyalty is not a virtue I take for granted, even from my background and training, and it is so refreshing to see it on display during the terrible times of Katrina. There is indeed a difference between hiring performers and athletes that are fantastic in their output, and having someone who will be around you no matter what, and buy into your vision, running with it like it is his or hers. That was the kind of people I had as staff coaches. They were people who would work with you because they see your success and failure as their own.

At the time, all I wanted to do was make a difference with the children in my care. I just wanted to communicate to them that they were deeply loved and would be cared for. I needed to let them know that they needed to graduate and excel beyond every barrier that stood in their way. I needed to tell them that they were in one of the best programs the world could offer, and to teach them the apparent distinction between talent and hard work, and what would come out of using them right and putting both of them in the proper perspective.

Coach Ellis even had two young kids at the time and took time off his fatherly duties to be with us, with the unwavering support of his wife. He would leave his young family to be with us to help out with a lot of stuff. Leaving his wife and kids to help us in such times isn't easy, and I appreciate his efforts a great deal. He would come around back and forth from New Orleans to help out with training the short spinners and the jumpers, as well as putting in lots of effort with the recruitment process. He was like a father to the group, and I am sure he was also excited to be a part of us. The fact that he didn't want any salary made it more inspiring for me, at a time when income was a significant motivation for doing most things.

Another remarkable character worthy of mention is Coach Jenkins, who was military, having put in some years in the Navy. He was the "discipline" man of the team, strong and well built. He had always had that reputation of sternness from our days at Belmont when he was one of my assistant coaches. He would not tolerate disobedience or recalcitrance of any sort and dealt with it on the spot. He was very prominent in holding the team together, and even though the team members sort of feared him, it was evident that they understood that he was acting in their best interests, and they loved him for it. I appreciate the level of compassion that made him stick with us and have so much belief in me at the time.

I can't forget the contributions of Coach Neil at the time. He was the brains behind the success of our long-distance runners, being a distance coach himself, who had just come in shortly before the crisis. He was very instrumental to our success in the championships that took place later in Coastal Carolina in the 5000 and 10000m categories. Apart from being the quintessential coach, he had a high level of motivational spirit, and his drive helped me during the times when my energy and motivation ran pretty low. He was always on hand to encourage me that I could take on any task. When I felt that I was too old to head the group, he would defeat the thought by saying very uplifting words. His energy and tenacity were out of this world, and he was a great pillar of strength at that time.

We were privileged to have facilities and material possessions that helped us through Hurricane Katrina.

But what helped us, even more, was the acceptance, love, and the relationships I cultivated and maintained with my team and the handlers. I saw so much love and cohesion in display in my inner circle, and when it seemed like I was going to fall apart and capitulate, they were always there to help me. Katrina was a defining moment in my life, and I doubt if there is any ugly event that can shake or shatter my faith in Christ, and what he is capable of doing for me.

Chapter 5

The Aftermath

Looking back and analyzing the events of the past years, especially the period surrounding Hurricane Katrina and the events in my life tied to it, I cannot help but appreciate God for His bountiful mercies in my life. Indeed, He has not only shown Himself strong but has also proven the veracity of Isaiah 40:31, which says that those that wait on the Lord shall renew their strength, mount up on wings like eagles and not be weary. Like I have mentioned previously, there is a difference between a faith you profess with your mouth and faith you practice actively. They are miles apart. During my mom's illness, I saw that difference on a whole new level, and I want as many people who would read my testimony to know that God is, and He is alive, watching and caring for you.

It was the Hurricane Irma season, and I cannot help but remember the events in that Katrina spell and reflect on what I have learned and how much I have grown since then, especially in love and in service to humanity. My stewardship to the people I worked with in Michigan ended sometime later, still on the aegis of standing for what was wrong and what was right. I was relieved of my appointment because there were certain life ideals I stood for that I could not compromise on. When I considered the injury to my integrity, apart from what a sin it was against God to compromise on some of my life principles, I concluded that it was better to let go of temporary fame and laurels for the greater good. This gave me peace of mind, both with myself and with my God. It did not go down well with my employers who did not see it the same way, and as was customary with such employers, soon, something trivial was cooked up against me, and that served as a convenient platform to send me packing. It did not bother me much, even though I was out of work for a considerably extended period, and yet again, my trust in God made sure I neither starved nor lacked. Instead, I began to get private clients whom I coached on my own, which paid better, or sometimes close to what I was getting previously. People would decide to foot my bills on their own accord, not knowing what I was going through at the time.

I will always appreciate what God used my mom to

do in my life and the lives of the four of us. Also, I must add here that there are specific experiences in life you would have concerning your walk with God that no pastor or religious figure would instill in you. You have to figure things for yourself and overcome. At that point in my life, I could easily follow the opinions of my siblings, but I was sure of what I believed in, and most importantly, the God I trusted. I was ready to go to any length to demonstrate that belief, and it paid off in the end. Even though some years later, it was time for my mom to pass away, she made more impact during that latter part of her life, and the testimony of her healing still rings loud and true to encourage people till today.

I also learned the truth about God's purpose for one's life. I learned that God is too deliberate to create someone by mistake, to exist for the sake of adding one more person to Earth. There is a deeper purpose for the creation of every human. It is left for the individual to discover it and live for that purpose. There might be obstacles and hindrances to that purpose, but with persistence and a clear direction of what it is, one would get there and function in that purpose. I feel so fulfilled coaching youngsters on track and field events that I almost think it is my purpose on Earth. Encouraging and giving them the best in me comes out effortlessly, and I keep seeing the impact it makes and how far they go in competitions.

Apart from that, returning to New Orleans and reflecting on the events of that period, I will appreciate the need for more love and accommodation in the world. During that time, I saw how the people from whom you would expect the most love were the ones who would appear to be the most bereft of it. The churches and religious outfits from whom I expected the most effort at rehabilitating the people were not there in the measure I expected. It would seem that the definition of Christianity these days is one of convenience and not a conviction; conviction of the responsibility imposed on Christians; conviction that the religion was not one to be verbalized, but one to be practice.

What would this world be like if we just stopped and did what was right vs. what was safe? Why are the churches closed to help during hard times, and only open during times it's convenient for them? The body of Christ was to help the helpless, hurt, wounded, and sick, lost, etc. Now, it is just the opposite; it's a business and corporation that God is not pleased with at all.

For many years to come, this season will always strike a chord in me, especially in the life-changing way it happened back in 2005. I am happier, more fulfilled, and a better man for that incident. My closing remarks would be the need for us to be more loving and accommodating of one another. Share love whenever you can, and in any capacity you find yourself. You might not know how far-reaching it would be. God, our Father, would pay no regard to one's race or color on the Day of Judgment. What would count ultimately would be how many lives one had been able to impact during the individual's stay on Earth.

Again, for a child of God, trust in God is not negotiable. For you to succeed and make a dramatic impact, it is compulsory. The more you are willing to trust God, the more He is ready to show you what it can earn you. I went through grueling periods of my life when it would seem like trusting God was brazen foolishness, to the level that depression was even threatening me, but the justification I got from it, made it all worth it in the end. I have become a sort of rallying point in my family at present, and this is the product of pure trust in God and nothing more. This is why the Bible aptly states in Proverbs 3:5-6,

Trust in the Lord with all thine heart, and lean not unto thine understanding. In all thy ways acknowledge Him, and He will direct thy paths.

I saw this scripture come alive during my trying moments, and I urge everyone to tap into it.

Trust in God always, and you cannot be put to shame. May God do for you what you cannot do for yourself.

Willie Randolph

University of New Orleans Outdoor Team

University Of New Orleans Farewell Tour

University Of New Orleans Winning Grambling Meet

University Of New Orleans Hurdles Practice

University Of New Orleans (Jasmine & Diana)

University Of New Orleans (Mike & Frank)

University Of New Orleans Team Dinner

St Albans Church (Coleena)

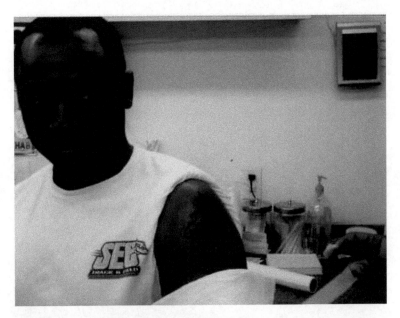

University Of New Orleans (Tattoo)

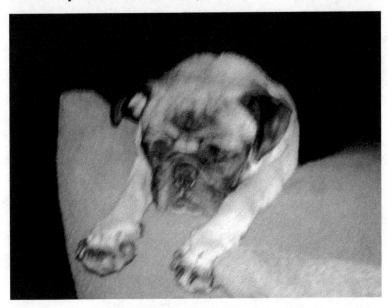

University Of New Orleans (Team Dog: **Lilly**)

Summary

2005 was a year that everything seemed to be in place. As a New Head coach at the University of New Orleans (UNO) I could never have imagined how much my life was about to change professionally and personally.

I had my new assistant coaches in place and we were ready to take on the world. Glen Jenkins , Trent Ellis, Chris Neal where all ready to begin a year that we all hoped would be the year to remember for our program. None of us knew it would be just that ... a year to remember. After the first 3 years it was hard trying to create and develop a program that had known very little success. However, in 2005 we had a nucleus of talent that would make a mark like no other track team at UNO.

We had support, but not that much support. The thing I didn't want was for anyone to not see our hard work, dedication, commitment to excellence pass by for any reason. Why, because excellence was built into my foundation to always give my best no matter what. I knew if I worked as unto pleasing God all would fall into place. Well, that year all of our Faiths would be tested to another level.

The level that we went to get athletes from across the globe extended all the way to Zimbabwe, Uganda, France , the Netherlands, Jamaica , Trinidad and Tobago, Grenada, and the list goes on. Having such a diverse group of athletes on our team would bring a challenge in itself, simply figuring out how to keep everyone working together as one team. The good days, bad days, the fears, the ability to eat, the loss of clothing would all turn our jobs into parents, and not just coaches. Again, we knew that in our hearts it was a challenge that we were ready to take on. We took it on as people loving people and not coaches just trying to get our athletes to perform.

Coming from my mother's foundation of keeping God first and treating everyone the way you want to be treated was cemented in my being for my entire life. These two things were pillars of my character. Going into 2005 the following athletes had a major impact on my life: Omar Smith , Kwesi , Nadia, Terrance Wills, Florant Frenchie, Vicki Howard, Diana J, Frank B, Juan Chapa, Jasmine Flournoy, Kyle , Pricilla Chapu , Angela Makaha, Itohan, Itty , Ramon G, Rayon, Kirk Anderson, Chris Sawyer, Bradley Rose, Robert Delmore,Jameel Wilson, Cory Denstal,

Jeff Draggich, Kip Fellon, Orion Wilson , Terrica Hamilton, and Coleena Collins. These students would become a part of my life, they would become my family that I swore I would protect and make sure they graduated from college. By the grace of God all of them would graduate and go on to be contributing factors to their communities.

One of the most amazing things that I have ever experienced in my life, was when we got word that UNO used their budget to make sure that the Basketball teams and baseball teams were safe from the storm by sending them to Tyler Texas. Once on Tyler a small community college would house the teams and make sure the student athletes were safe. It would be weeks later until UNO would find our track team and ask me to connect them with the LSU athletic department. Through my connection with my dear friend Eddie Nunez a former co-worker from LSU, we were able to secure a place for our team to practice on a weekly basis and still attend classes as visiting students at LSU.

The overall goal was to stay together as a family and to stay together as a unit! A group of people with a collective goal to do everything as a family. We even ate all of our meals together that my staff and I cooked together. Without the foundation from my mother that began with Unconditional Love, I could have easily just thought of myself, left the students, and went to safety on my on. Yet, I learned it wasn't about the storm that caused me to think about who I was, it was the people around me, and the fact that they believed in me and my staff to hold their futures together. It kept me moving as a coach, it made me think daily that I must treat these kids the way I wanted to be treated even if it cost me my life. With the support of Trent Ellis, Chris Neal , Glen Jenkins I knew that we could and would make it through the adversity. The fact that we 4 were able to stay and live together in a small house the entire fall and not kill each other was in itself another one of God's miracles.

In this book the goal is to show everyone some of the keys we used to survive Katrina. Faced with fear, abandonment, and many other obstacles getting through the other side of it all was nothing short of a miracle. This is my testimony of what we can do as a human race if we Keep God first, and Love each other equally. "Faith in the Eye of the Storm."

Coach's Quotes:

Trent Ellis - UNO Jumps Coach

"It was a humbling experience, because so many people on the team were non-Louisianans so what was coming wasn't taken seriously. So there was a last minute dash to get out which caused lots of angst and stress. People were trying to collect things from all over, fortunately everyone made it to Baton Rouge safely. Coming out of it our coaches and team grew closer, and till this day I have that same close relationship with many of the athletes. Through social media we are able to communicate and stay in touch.

We helped each other to get through the adversity of the storm. For the remainder of the school year we relocated the students to LSU. Several schools reached out and provided clothing and shoes for our student athletes and this gesture made me realize that the sport of track and field was one big community. Even though we compete each other we stick together to help student athletes in need. Through the generosity of others we made it safely through the storm.

I have not openly talked about that time until now, but I will never forget the looks, the expressions, and the feelings of the team knowing that everything they had was gone. All was gone except God."

Chris Neal - UNO Distance Coach

"The Katrina year was like no year I have ever had as a coach. However, as a young coach I think it helped me to grow up very fast. All our staff had was each other and our team. I felt like from top to bottom everyone rose to the challenge to have one of the best seasons in UNO history."

About the Author

I'm a Black Man/ African American, as well as Choctaw Indian, and Cherokee living in a world of daily challenges like everyone else. Although, I'm most humbled to be the First Black male in my family to graduate in three generations, I'm a man who Loves God with all his heart, mind, body and soul. Also, while on this journey I've grown to recognize that we each have flaws that we must deal with over the course of our lives in our own way. Therefore, my deep belief in Gods sovereignty, Love ,Grace and Mercy is the center piece of my life that I share with you.

I was raised by a single mom, the youngest of 4 in a small town called Saginaw Michigan.   Born Willie Randolph Jr. The son of now deceased dad Willie Randolph I never grew up with a dad, but was raised by my mother's Venus Weston, dad and mother when she was away at work. Therefore, I was grounded in a lot of   wisdom that gave me an Old Soul, as many would call it today.

I am a collegiate Track And Field coach who has been blessed to start my twenty third year of Coaching Division I Track and Field.   I've gone through social media attempts of destroying my character for standing up for what was right. I've lost a dream job, and have been passed over for jobs that I know I was equally qualified or overqualified for. Yet, being a black man in America has always felt like I had to explain why speaking correct English was not white, but it simply Right.

However , out of all my accomplishments, loses, and struggles in life I'm most grateful for my FAITH in God and the gift of a strong Mother who raised me into the diverse man I am today.   Not only did she raise me, but she opened my eyes to many villages of people that helped shape my view of Life, Faith, Love and the world. She always reminded me that there is always someone watching how you deal with Adversity and Life, but most of all you must keep God first, Pray, and keep your FAITH. Therefore, I truly pray this book helps others to learn how to guard their MIND, Body and Soul as I Willie Randolph continue to try to do the same with God's Grace and Mercy.

Acknowledgements

I would to thank Thomas M. Hickey, Craig Littlepage, Mr. Paul Novak, Mr. Almon W Gunter Jr. for their tireless support and mentorship over the years.

CPSIA information can be obtained
at www.ICGtesting.com
Printed in the USA
LVHW010851100721
692198LV00012B/882